SOUL

A Personalized Guide to

Deepen Your Lenten Faith

Experience

Rev. Fr. Joshua M. Tillman

COPYRIGHT PAGE

All rights reserved. No part of this publication may be reproduced in any form or means without prior written permission from the copyright holder.

Copyright ©2023 Rev. Fr. Joshua M. Tillman

Acknowledgments

I express my deepest appreciation to those who have contributed to the creation of this guide. May your Lenten experience be enriched and your spirit uplifted.

Table of Contents

INTRODUCTION 8

   BRIEF OVERVIEW OF LENT AND ITS SIGNIFICANCE:..........15

   INVITATION TO PERSONAL REFLECTION AND SPIRITUAL GROWTH: 16

   HOW TO USE THE BOOK: A GUIDE FOR READERS: 18

CHAPTER 1: THE PRELUDE - UNDERSTANDING LENT 21

   EXPLORING THE THEOLOGY OF LENT: 22

   HISTORICAL CONTEXT AND TRADITIONS: 23

   THE PURPOSE OF FASTING, PRAYER, AND ALMSGIVING: ..24

   SETTING PERSONAL INTENTIONS FOR THE LENTEN SEASON: 26

CHAPTER 2: HARMONY OF THE HEART - PRAYER AND CONTEMPLATION 28

   CRAFTING MEANINGFUL PRAYERS:...............................29

INCORPORATING SCRIPTURAL REFLECTIONS: 30

PERSONAL PRAYER JOURNALING: 33

LENTEN PRAYERS 35

A Prayer of Surrender: 35

A Prayer of Gratitude:.....................................35

A Prayer of Reflection: 36

A Prayer for Silence:.......................................37

A Prayer for Contemplation: 38

A Prayer of Intention:.....................................38

A Prayer for Unity: 39

A Prayer for Healing:......................................40

A Prayer for Wisdom:.....................................40

A Prayer for Divine Presence:.........................41

CHAPTER 3: NOURISHING THE SOUL - FASTING

WITH PURPOSE 42

TYPES OF FASTING IN CATHOLIC TRADITION: 43

THE SPIRITUAL SIGNIFICANCE OF FASTING: 44

BALANCING PHYSICAL AND SPIRITUAL NUTRITION: 46

CREATING PERSONALIZED FASTING PRACTICES: 47

CHAPTER 4: ACTS OF LOVE - ALMSGIVING AND COMMUNITY ENGAGEMENT 49

UNDERSTANDING ALMSGIVING IN A MODERN CONTEXT:.50

THE INTERSECTION OF CHARITY AND SOCIAL JUSTICE: 51

BUILDING A COMMUNITY OF SUPPORT AND ACCOUNTABILITY: 53

PRACTICAL ACTS OF LOVE AND KINDNESS: 54

CHAPTER 5: THE LENTEN PILGRIMAGE - RITUALS AND PRACTICES..57

PARTICIPATING IN LENTEN LITURGIES AND SERVICES: 58

ENGAGING IN TRADITIONAL PRACTICES (STATIONS OF THE CROSS, ROSARY, ETC.): 59

INCORPORATING SYMBOLISM INTO DAILY LIFE:..............60

CREATING A HOME ALTAR FOR LENT: 62

CHAPTER 6: TRANSFORMATIVE REFLECTIONS - A JOURNEY WITHIN 64

Reflecting on Personal Growth and Transformation: 65

Celebrating Achievements and Overcoming Challenges: 66

Integrating Lenten Lessons into Everyday Life: 68

Preparing for the Joy of Easter: 69

CONCLUSION 71

Introduction

In the tapestry of life, we often find ourselves grappling with the complexities of faith, yearning for a more meaningful connection with the Divine. Perhaps you, like many others, have felt the ache of a spiritual longing, the yearning for a deeper encounter with God that transcends routine practices and reaches the core of your soul.

In the hustle of our modern lives, the sacred season of Lent often becomes a mere ritual—a checklist of religious duties without a true understanding of its transformative potential. As a compassionate advocate for social justice, I have witnessed the yearning for a spirituality that goes beyond the surface, one that addresses the profound challenges we face in our hearts and the world.

This book is born from the recognition of those challenges, a recognition that the sacred journey of Lent can be a powerful remedy for the spiritual malaise that so often afflicts us. As you navigate these pages, envision a future where your Lenten experience becomes a beacon of hope, guiding you toward a faith that is vibrant, personal, and deeply resonant.

Through "Soulful Lent," you will embark on a journey of self-discovery, exploring the nuances of theology, prayer, fasting, almsgiving, rituals, and transformative reflections. It is a guide designed not only to lead you through the rituals of the season but to help you uncover the profound spiritual truths that lie beneath the surface.

As a Catholic priest with a deep commitment to the spiritual welfare of my parishioners, I've witnessed firsthand the transformative power of a soulful Lenten experience. I've seen lives changed, hearts softened, and spirits uplifted through intentional and personalized engagement with the Lenten journey.

So, why should you commit to reading this entire book? Within these pages, you will find the keys to unlock the dormant potential of your Lenten experience. You will discover how to turn the challenges of faith into opportunities for growth, and you will learn to infuse your spiritual practices with a vitality that resonates with the love and compassion of Christ.

Join me on this journey. Let "Soulful Lent" be your companion as you navigate the sacred season and emerge with a spirit that is truly resurrected. The challenges you face can be transformed into stepping stones toward a more profound and meaningful connection with God. It's time to embark on a soulful pilgrimage—one that leads you not only through Lent but beyond, into a future where your faith is vibrant, your spirit is uplifted, and your soul resonates with the eternal joy of Easter.

Brief Overview of Lent and Its Significance:

Lent, a season of forty days preceding Easter, holds profound significance in the Christian tradition. It is a time of preparation, self-examination, and a journey toward the celebration of Christ's resurrection. During Lent, we follow in the footsteps of Jesus, reflecting on His sacrifice and contemplating our spiritual paths.

In this sacred season, we engage in practices such as fasting, prayer, and almsgiving, seeking to deepen our connection with God and embrace a life of greater purpose and compassion.

Invitation to Personal Reflection and Spiritual Growth:

As you delve into the pages of "Soulful Lent," we invite you to embark on a deeply personal journey. This is more than a book; it's a guide tailored to help you discover the unique contours of your spiritual landscape. Embrace this opportunity for self-discovery, inviting the transformative power of Lent to touch your heart and soul.

Allow these words to be a companion on your journey, encouraging introspection, guiding you through moments of prayerful contemplation, and inspiring acts of kindness and charity.

How to Use the Book: A Guide for Readers:

Before you begin, take a moment to familiarize yourself with how this guide is structured:

Introduction: Gain insights into the purpose of Lent and the approach of this guide.

Chapters 1-5: Explore different facets of Lent, including

understanding its theology, deepening prayer, purposeful fasting, acts of love through almsgiving, and engaging in rituals and practices.

Chapter 6: Reflect on the transformative journey within, celebrating personal growth and preparing for Easter joy.

Conclusion: Summarize the Lenten experience and consider how to carry its lessons forward.

Feel free to personalize your journey by journaling in the

spaces provided, making this guide uniquely yours.

May "Soulful Lent" be a source of inspiration, guidance, and spiritual nourishment as you navigate the sacred season ahead.

Warmest regards,

Rev. Fr. Joshua M. Tillman

Chapter 1: The Prelude - Understanding Lent

In the hush of anticipation, we stand on the threshold of Lent—a season of profound significance. In this chapter, we lay the foundation for your Lenten journey by exploring the theology, traditions, and purpose behind these sacred forty days.

Exploring the Theology of Lent:

Lent is not merely a period on the liturgical calendar; it is a theological voyage inviting us to delve into the heart of our faith. Explore the theological underpinnings of Lent—its roots in the desert experiences of biblical figures, its connection to the Passion of Christ, and the invitation to spiritual renewal. As we understand the theological tapestry, we pave the way for a richer and more intentional Lenten experience.

Historical Context and Traditions:

Unravel the tapestry of time as we delve into the historical context of Lent and the traditions that have shaped it. From its early beginnings in the early Christian Church to the varied practices across denominations, discover how Lent has evolved into the multifaceted and revered season we observe today. Understanding the historical context enriches our appreciation for the traditions that bind us to generations of believers.

The Purpose of Fasting, Prayer, and Almsgiving:

Why do we fast, pray, and give alms during Lent? In this section, we delve into the purpose behind these practices. Fasting is not a mere abstention from food; it is a spiritual discipline that heightens our awareness and dependence on God. Prayer becomes a lifeline, connecting us to the Divine. Almsgiving extends beyond charity; it is an expression of love and solidarity with those in need. Understanding the profound purpose behind these actions transforms them into meaningful steps on our Lenten journey.

Setting Personal Intentions for the Lenten Season:

Lent is a personal pilgrimage, a unique journey for each soul. In this section, we guide you in setting your intentions for the season. What areas of your life need attention and renewal? What spiritual goals do you hope to achieve? Reflect on these questions and craft personal intentions that resonate with your unique path. As we set our sights on the journey ahead, these intentions become guiding stars, illuminating the way through the Lenten wilderness.

As you conclude this chapter, may you carry with you a deeper understanding of Lent, its theological roots, historical significance, and the purpose behind the practices that define this sacred season. As you turn the page, step into the heart of Lent with intention and purpose.

Chapter 2: Harmony of the Heart - Prayer and Contemplation

In the sacred space of prayer, we find harmony—where the soul's melody blends with the divine symphony. This chapter invites you to explore the art of crafting meaningful prayers, embracing scriptural reflections, discovering the power of silence, and engaging in contemplative practices that resonate with the rhythm of your heart.

Crafting Meaningful Prayers:

Prayer is the language of the soul, a dialogue between the finite and the infinite. In this section, we explore the art of crafting prayers that resonate with the depths of your being. Learn to express gratitude, seek guidance, and offer contrition with sincerity. Discover the beauty of spontaneous conversation with the Divine, forging a connection that transforms your Lenten journey into a profound conversation with God.

Incorporating Scriptural Reflections:

Scripture is a wellspring of wisdom, a source of inspiration that breathes life into our prayers. Explore the transformative power of incorporating scriptural reflections into your daily devotions. Discover passages that align with the themes of Lent, providing a foundation for contemplation and guiding your reflections. As you immerse yourself in the sacred text, let it become a companion on your journey, offering insights and revelations.

The Power of Silence and Contemplative Practices:

In the stillness of silence, we encounter the Divine. Delve into the transformative power of silence and contemplative practices during Lent. Explore techniques that quiet the noise of the world, creating space for God's whispers to be heard. Whether through meditation, mindfulness, or intentional moments of quiet, discover the harmony that arises when the heart finds solace in silence.

Personal Prayer Journaling:

A personal Lenten journey deserves a personal record. In this section, we encourage you to embark on the practice of personal prayer journaling. Capture your thoughts, feelings, and experiences as you navigate the Lenten landscape. Document your prayers, reflections, and the divine encounters that shape your spiritual path. Your journal becomes a sacred space where the journey unfolds, and your soul's melody is penned on the pages of your heart.

Lenten Prayers

A Prayer of Surrender:
Heavenly Father, in the quiet moments of this Lenten journey, I surrender my heart to Your divine presence. May the symphony of my soul harmonize with Your will, and may my prayers rise like incense, sweet and pleasing in Your sight.

A Prayer of Gratitude:
Gracious God, as I craft my prayers, let the melody of

gratitude flow from my heart. In the stillness, help me recognize the countless blessings woven into the tapestry of my life. I offer thanks for the gift of this Lenten season and the opportunity to draw closer to You.

A Prayer of Reflection:
Lord, as I reflect on Your Word, guide my thoughts and open my heart to the messages You have for me. May the sacred verses become a lantern on my Lenten

path, illuminating the way to deeper understanding and spiritual growth.

A Prayer for Silence:
God of Peace, in the hush of silence, I seek Your presence. Quiet the noise around me and within me, that I may hear the whispers of Your love. In this stillness, grant me a profound encounter with You.

A Prayer for Contemplation:

Eternal Wisdom, as I engage in contemplative practices, grant me insight and revelation. May the mysteries of faith unfold before me, and may my heart resonate with the profound truths hidden in the depths of Your love.

A Prayer of Intention:

Loving Father, as I craft my intentions for this Lenten season, guide me in setting my heart on things above. May my desires align with Your will, and may each prayerful intention draw me closer to the person You created me to be.

A Prayer for Unity:
Holy Spirit, in the tapestry of prayers woven by believers around the world, unite our hearts in a chorus of love and devotion. Though we are diverse, may our prayers create a harmonious symphony that rises

as a pleasing offering before Your throne.

A Prayer for Healing:
Merciful Healer, as I lift my prayers, I intercede for those who are in need of Your healing touch. Pour out Your grace on the broken, the hurting, and the weary. May the balm of Your love bring restoration and renewal.

A Prayer for Wisdom:

Divine Wisdom, as I delve into Your Word, grant me discernment and understanding. Illuminate my mind with the light of Your truth, that my prayers may be anchored in wisdom and guided by Your infinite knowledge.

A Prayer for Divine Presence:
Ever-Present God, as I enter the sacred space of prayer, I acknowledge Your nearness. May my contemplation be a meeting of hearts, where Your presence

transforms my inner being and brings about a sacred harmony in my soul.

Chapter 3: Nourishing the Soul - Fasting with Purpose

In the delicate balance between fasting and nourishment, we discover a profound journey of self-discipline and spiritual growth. This chapter invites you to explore the diverse types of fasting in the Catholic tradition, unravel the spiritual significance of fasting, strike a harmonious balance between physical and spiritual nutrition, and craft personalized fasting practices that resonate with the essence of your Lenten pilgrimage.

Types of Fasting in Catholic Tradition:

The Catholic tradition embraces a spectrum of fasting practices, each offering a unique path for spiritual discipline. Explore the various types of fasting observed during Lent, from abstaining from certain foods to limiting meal sizes. Delve into the ancient traditions that have shaped the Lenten fasting landscape, and consider which approach aligns with your journey of self-discipline and spiritual reflection.

The Spiritual Significance of Fasting:

Fasting is more than a physical act of abstaining; it is a spiritual discipline that deepens our connection with God. Uncover the profound spiritual significance of fasting as it relates to Lent. By denying ourselves in a specific area, we create space for spiritual nourishment. Discover how fasting becomes a sacred journey, allowing us to attune our hearts to the rhythms of prayer, self-reflection, and a heightened awareness of God's presence.

Balancing Physical and Spiritual Nutrition:

As we fast during Lent, it's crucial to strike a delicate balance between physical and spiritual nutrition. In this section, explore practical ways to nourish your body while honoring the spiritual discipline of fasting. Embrace nutrient-dense foods that sustain your physical well-being and, at the same time, consider how your dietary choices can contribute to a heightened spiritual awareness.

The harmony between physical and spiritual nutrition becomes a key aspect of your soulful Lenten experience.

Creating Personalized Fasting Practices:

Lent is a personal journey, and fasting is a deeply personal practice. In this part, discover the art of crafting personalized fasting practices that align with your spiritual goals and physical well-being. Tailor your fast to your unique circumstances, taking into consideration your health, lifestyle, and the aspects of your life that require intentional focus. By personalizing your fasting practices, you transform this Lenten discipline into a meaningful and sustainable expression of your commitment to spiritual growth.

Chapter 4: Acts of Love - Almsgiving and Community Engagement

In the generous spirit of Lent, we embark on a chapter devoted to acts of love—embracing the modern context of almsgiving, exploring the intersection of charity and social justice, building a community of support and accountability, and engaging in practical acts of love and kindness that echo the compassion of Christ.

Understanding Almsgiving in a Modern Context:

Almsgiving transcends the mere act of giving; it's a profound expression of love and compassion. In this section, we explore the modern context of almsgiving, understanding how it goes beyond material donations. Explore the ways in which you can contribute to the well-being of others, whether through financial support, time, or resources. As you navigate the landscape of almsgiving, discover how your generosity can bring about meaningful change in the lives of those in need.

The Intersection of Charity and Social Justice:

Charity and social justice are intertwined threads in the fabric of almsgiving. Delve into the deeper dimensions of your acts of love, exploring how they intersect with the principles of social justice. Through your generosity, become an advocate for positive change, addressing systemic issues and promoting a more just and compassionate society. In this Lenten season, may your acts of love reverberate beyond individual charity, creating ripples of justice and equality.

Building a Community of Support and Accountability:

Almsgiving is a communal endeavor that flourishes in the rich soil of community. In this part, explore the importance of building a community of support and accountability. Engage with others who share a common commitment to acts of love and create a network that fosters encouragement and accountability. Together, as a community, amplify the impact of your collective acts of kindness and create a supportive environment that nurtures spiritual growth.

Practical Acts of Love and Kindness:

Love finds its expression in practical deeds. In this section, discover tangible and practical acts of love and kindness that resonate with the heart of Christ.

From small daily gestures to larger community initiatives, explore ways to infuse love into the fabric of your daily life. Through these acts, may you become a living testament to the transformative power of love, kindness, and compassion during the Lenten season.

As you engage in acts of love, may the spirit of almsgiving permeate your soul, creating a tapestry of compassion and kindness that reflects the love of Christ. In the modern context of almsgiving, may your generosity become a powerful force for positive change, both individually and within the broader community.

Chapter 5: The Lenten Pilgrimage - Rituals and Practices

Embark on a sacred pilgrimage as we explore the rich tapestry of Lenten rituals and practices. In this chapter, discover the transformative power of participating in liturgies, engaging in timeless traditions, infusing symbolism into your daily life, and creating a sacred space with a home altar for Lent.

Participating in Lenten Liturgies and Services:

The liturgical season of Lent offers a unique opportunity to engage in communal worship and reflection. In this section, explore the profound impact of participating in Lenten liturgies and services. From Ash Wednesday to the solemnity of Good Friday, each service contributes to the collective journey of the faithful. Immerse yourself in the solemnity of these gatherings, allowing the liturgical rhythm to guide your Lenten pilgrimage.

Engaging in Traditional Practices (Stations of the Cross, Rosary, etc.):

Tradition weaves a thread that connects us to the faithful who have gone before. Delve into the beauty of traditional Lenten practices, such as the Stations of the Cross and the Rosary. Each station becomes a step on your pilgrimage, and each bead of the Rosary is a whispered prayer. Discover the timeless nature of these practices, allowing them to be a guide through the Lenten landscape and a source of reflection on Christ's journey to Calvary.

Incorporating Symbolism into Daily Life:

Symbolism has the power to infuse the ordinary with the extraordinary. In this section, learn to incorporate symbolism into your daily life throughout the Lenten season. Whether through visual symbols, intentional acts, or symbolic fasting, discover how these practices deepen your connection to the spiritual significance of Lent. As you navigate your day, may each symbol serve as a poignant reminder of your Lenten commitment and the transformative power of the season.

Creating a Home Altar for Lent:

Your home can become a sacred sanctuary during Lent through the creation of a home altar. In this part, explore the meaningful process of designing and crafting a space that serves as a focal point for prayer and reflection. Choose symbols and elements that resonate with the Lenten journey, creating an environment that nurtures your spiritual growth. Whether simple or elaborate, your home altar becomes a tangible expression of your commitment to a soulful Lenten pilgrimage.

Chapter 6: Transformative Reflections - A Journey Within

In the quiet spaces of reflection, we uncover the transformative power of our Lenten journey. This chapter invites you to look within, reflecting on personal growth and transformation, celebrating achievements, overcoming challenges, integrating Lenten lessons into everyday life, and preparing your heart for the joy of Easter.

Reflecting on Personal Growth and Transformation:

As Lent draws to a close, take a moment to reflect on the journey within. Explore how this season has nurtured personal growth and transformation. Delve into the insights gained through prayer, fasting, almsgiving, and engagement with spiritual practices. Recognize the subtle shifts in your soul, acknowledging the seeds of change that have been planted during this sacred season.

Celebrating Achievements and Overcoming Challenges:

In this section, celebrate the achievements and milestones reached on your Lenten pilgrimage. Acknowledge the discipline of fasting, the generosity of almsgiving, and the depth of your prayers. Equally, recognize the challenges faced and overcome. Reflect on the lessons learned through struggles, and embrace the resilience that has been cultivated. In this Lenten journey, every step forward is a cause for celebration.

Integrating Lenten Lessons into Everyday Life:

The lessons of Lent are not confined to a season; they are meant to permeate every aspect of our lives. Explore ways to integrate the profound insights gained during Lent into your daily routine. Whether through continued prayer practices, sustained acts of kindness, or a mindful approach to living, discover how the lessons of Lent can shape your character and guide your choices beyond this sacred season.

Preparing for the Joy of Easter:

As Easter approaches, prepare your heart for the joyous celebration of resurrection and new life. In this part, consider the spiritual significance of Easter and the joy it brings. Reflect on the resurrection as a symbol of hope and renewal, and anticipate the joy that springs forth from the transformative work of Lent. As you stand at the threshold of Easter, let your heart be filled with anticipation and gratitude for the journey within.

Conclusion

Resurrected Spirit - Beyond Lent

As we draw the curtain on the sacred season of Lent, we stand at the threshold of renewal, transformed by the journey within. This conclusion marks not an end but a continuation—a perpetual journey of spiritual growth, deepened faith, and a resurrected spirit.

Summarizing the Lenten Journey:

In the chapters preceding this conclusion, you've explored the multifaceted landscape of Lent—embracing theology, prayer, fasting, almsgiving, rituals, and transformative reflections. Each facet has woven a unique thread into the tapestry of your Lenten journey, creating a mosaic of spiritual experiences and insights.

Emphasizing the Importance of Continuous Spiritual Growth:

As we bid farewell to the specific disciplines of Lent, let us carry forward the spirit of intentional living and spiritual growth. Beyond the confines of this season, may our commitment to prayer, acts of love, and reflection endure, shaping our character and deepening our connection with the Divine.

Encouraging Ongoing Practices Beyond Lent:

The conclusion of Lent is not the conclusion of our spiritual journey. Let the disciplines embraced during this season become enduring practices in our lives. Whether in moments of quiet prayer, acts of kindness, or ongoing reflection, may the soulful essence of Lent remain a guiding force in our daily existence.

Expressing Gratitude and Hope for the Future:

Gratitude fills our hearts as we reflect on the transformative journey shared in these pages. We express our deepest thanks for your companionship, for allowing "Soulful Lent" to be a part of your spiritual pilgrimage.

As you move beyond these words, may your heart resonate with hope—a hope that springs eternal, rooted in the promise of resurrection and the enduring love of the Divine.

In conclusion, "Soulful Lent" is not merely a guide for a season; it's an invitation to a lifelong journey of faith, love, and growth. May the lessons learned and the practices embraced during Lent continue to bear fruit in the seasons to come. As we step into the future, may our spirits be forever resurrected, and may the joy of Easter be a constant companion on our journey toward a deeper, more meaningful connection with God.

Warmest regards,

Rev. Fr. Joshua M. Tillman

Printed in Great Britain
by Amazon